# Tapas

# Tapas

## Marie McDonald

NEW HOLLAND

Dedicated to my wonderful mother Iris Hayward McDonald

# Acknowledgements

Thank you to all the chefs, cooks and kitchen staff who have created tapas before me and given me the self belief that I also could sauté, fry, roast, bake, grill, chill, heat and combine food ingredients into something wonderful to offer customers in our restaurant.

I would like to thank Rick Stockdale for the encouragement and praise he has given me in the creation of this book.

Thanks goes to my daughter Jessie for the long hours she has spent with me in our kitchen—her support in this venture is forever treasured.

Thanks to Chef Linda Johns, who from day one brought to my kitchen the systems that I use everyday. Thanks also to my numerous kitchen staff that have worked day in and day out, have come and gone and sometimes have come back to my kitchen over the four years we have been serving tapas at Brandy Creek Wines and View Café.

I would also like to thank Chef Jose Castro for the inspiration he gives me every day and for the wonderful dishes he creates for us and our customers to enjoy.

Finally I would like to thank the many thousands of customers who have enjoyed our tapas. Their delight at discovering the pleasures of the 'tasty little dishes from Spain', the kind comments they have made to me and my staff and their positive recommendations they have made to their friends and family have been both humbling and inspirational.

# contents

contents

A group of four friends have just arrived at the cellar door restaurant for lunch. They were met at the door by one of our staff and have been seated at a table at the front of our alfresco balcony. It's a warm sunny day but they are delightfully shaded by the canopy of the grape vine growing across the top of the patio. The vineyard, cellar door and restaurant are situated on a gentle, elevated north-facing slope. The view is magnificent—always green, overlooking some of our vineyard, our olive grove, neighbouring farms and out to the Baw Baw ranges in the distance.

One of the guests murmurs, 'It's just like Provence or Tuscany where we were last winter, remember?'

I hand each of them a flute. 'I thought you might like to start your visit with a tasting of our Sparkling Pinot Gris. This is made the same way that Champagne is made. It is an early disgorged style that is light and crisp, while retaining many of the fruit characteristics. It is an excellent aperitif and celebratory wine. Please enjoy your stay at Brandy Creek Wines.' I point out the vines which produced the grapes for the Sparkling Pinot Gris.

As I leave the table the sounds of a toast, the clink of glasses and the exclamations of delight at how good the wine is mingle with the satisfying buzz of a restaurant full of people having a really good time as they experience the delicious flavours of Marie's Tapas menu and our wines. This makes it all worthwhile. The happy sounds and feelings of our visitors having a fantastic experience is a great reward for the passion, dedication, hard work, training and careful planning myself, Marie, and our staff have put into what we have created at Brandy Creek Wines & View Café.

We bought the small acreage property, which is situated on Buln Buln Road, Camp Hill at Brandy Creek near Warragul in West Gippsland Victoria, in

1996. It is easily accessible from Melbourne, just off the Princess Highway (M1) less than an hour's drive from the south-eastern suburbs.

The existing property had been part of a larger dairy farm. Down the hill from the current house (built by the previous owner) is the site of the original dairy farmer's cottage. We still find old bottles or kitchen utensils from the site. One of our regular customers was born in the house. He tells us that his parents dragged it overland by horse-drawn sled in the early 1900s, from the old abandoned gold-mining town of Walhalla. Some feat—a journey of more than 60 kilometres over some pretty steep terrain with only dirt tracks at best.

We bought another four acres of land from a neighbour, and over a period of three years planted about five acres (two hectares) of grapes roughly 50 per cent each of Tempranillo (a Spanish red wine variety) and Pinot Gris (a French white wine variety), with a few rows of Pinot Meunier.

The 2004 crop was sufficient for a commercial vintage. It takes about 18 months for wines requiring barrel conditioning to be ready to drink. We spent the time building the cellar door/restaurant.

Our selected food style was Spanish Tapas made from local fresh ingredients. There was synergy with the Tempranillo grape variety we were growing, it is a relaxed style supporting the ambience we wished to create and the many small different tasting dishes went with wine tasting.

Finally we opened for business on the Sunday after the Melbourne Cup in November 2005. It became obvious within a few weeks that we had vastly underestimated the demand for our bold and innovative food and wine style. Within a year we had added a function room, taking our capacity to 130 visitors, upgraded the kitchen and employed many more people.

Our wines, made by Peter Beckingham, have won several awards and many medals. We are particularly proud of the Sparkling Pinot Gris.

There are three people whose contribution to the success of Brandy Creek Wines & View Café must be celebrated: Consultant chef Linda Johns, whose special skills in the kitchen in the early days were a foundation; and Draga Orwin, who managed the front of house for many years and provided an exceptionally high level of skill and service to that function. The real driving force behind the success of Brandy Creek Wines is Marie. It is her passion for food, her unrelenting hard work, her natural ability to know what will work and what won't, her persistence and determination to only receive and deliver perfection that brings people back to the restaurant time after time. We hope you enjoy creating these dishes in your own kitchen.

Rick Stockdale

# Morning Time

# Fried Eggs with Jamon

Serves 1

**2 slices stale bread**
**salt**
**oil for frying**
**2 eggs**
**2 slices jamon**
**chopped parsley**
**Romesco Sauce (see page 146)**

Cut the bread up into fingers, spread out on tray, spray with a little water until just damp and sprinkle with salt. Heat oil in a shallow pan and fry bread until crispy. Set aside.

Fry eggs in oil until whites are cooked.

Place bread on a plate, transfer eggs and jamon to the bread, sprinkle with parsley. Serve with Romesco Sauce.

# Asparagus with Quail Eggs

Serves 1

150g (5oz) green asparagus
150g (5oz) white asparagus
2 quail eggs
spring onion (shallot) strips
Piquillo Pepper Sauce (see page 148)
salt and pepper to taste

Peel the asparagus and only use the top one-third of the stalks.

Blanch the asparagus for about 2 minutes in boiling water, then plunge into ice cold water.

Boil the eggs for 2 minutes the drop them into cold water.

Tie the asparagus together using spring onion strips, then place on a plate. Gently pour the piquillo pepper sauce over the asparagus and onto the plate.

Peel the boiled eggs, and cut in half lengthwise, place on top of the sauce beside the asparagus, serve immediately.

# View Café Baked Beans

Serves 8

**2 cups large dried beans, soaked for 12–24 hours**
**extra virgin olive oil**
**1 brown onion, finely chopped**
**1 clove garlic, thinly sliced**
**½ bunch thyme**
**2 dried bay leaves**
**2 cups (500ml, 16fl oz) Chicken Stock (see page 144)**
**2½ cups (600ml, 20fl oz) Piperade (see page 151)**
**parsley to serve**

Place beans in a large ceramic bowl, cover with cold water and set aside for 12–24 hours to soak. Drain well, rinse and drain again.

Cover base of large frying pan with extra virgin olive oil and heat over high heat, add the beans, onion, garlic, thyme and bay leaves, stir to coat. Pour in the Chicken Stock and reduce, then add the Piperade. Reduce heat to low, cover and simmer for 2 hours or until beans are tender.

Taste the beans, adjust the seasoning as required. Sprinkle with parsley. Serve with fingers of toast.

Morning Tissue

# Piperade Beans with Baked Eggs & Chorizo

Serves 1

½ cup Piperade (see page 151)
½ cup Baked Beans (see page 17)
1 chorizo
2 medium-sized eggs

Preheat oven to 180ºC (350ºF, Gas Mark 4).

In a saucepan, heat the Piperade and baked beans over a low flame until hot. Slice and sauté chorizo in a shallow frying pan until brown, transfer to a cazuella or heat-proof dish. Spoon over Piperade and Baked Beans, crack in the eggs. Bake in oven for approximately 10 minutes, or until eggs are set.

Remove from oven. Serve immediately, with hot toasted bread.

# Saffron Yoghurt with Dates & Nuts

Serves 6

**250g (8oz) plain yoghurt**
**pinch saffron threads**
**2 tablespoons caster sugar**
**¼ teaspoon cardamom**
**2 teaspoons rosewater**
**3 fresh dates, pipped and cut into slivers**
**chopped walnuts**

Place yoghurt, saffron threads, caster sugar, cardamom and rosewater in a large bowl and mix together until all the ingredients are combined.

Take a new piece of muslin, rinse in hot water, wring out well and place in a small sieve or colander. Empty yoghurt into the cloth, fold over the edges and leave draining over a bowl in the fridge for most of a day or overnight.

Serve topped with slivered dates and chopped walnuts.

# Vegetables

# The Peppers of Padron

Serves 4

**olive oil for frying**
**250g (8oz) Padron capsicums (peppers)**
**flake salt to taste**

Put a few tablespoons of olive oil in a frying pan to heat. Fry the peppers over a high heat until blistered. Spoon onto a plate and sprinkle with the salt. Serve immediately.

**To Drink**
Sauvignon Blanc. Brandy Creek's popular 2008 Sauvignon Blanc features a grassy nose and a mineral taste that will diminish the heat from the peppers.

# Whole Mushrooms Glazed with Garlic & Sherry Vinegar

Serves 2

200g (7oz) button mushrooms
1 clove garlic, crushed
pinch rosemary
black pepper
salt
splash of oil
chopped parsley for garnish
a splash of sherry vinegar

Heat oil in a frying pan, toss in mushrooms, crushed garlic and rosemary and black pepper. Sauté for approximately 3 minutes until brown. Splash with sherry vinegar and season with salt to taste. Serve hot.

**To Drink**
Pinot Noir is great with any full-flavoured mushroom dish. Brandy Creek Wines 2007 variety features strong, spicy truffle, barnyard and earthy tones.

# Tortilla Espanola (Spanish Omelette)

Serves 8

**roasted bulb of garlic**
**splash of olive oil to garnish**
**1kg (2.2lb) Maris Piper potatoes, peeled and sliced**
**250ml (8fl oz) olive oil**
**6 large eggs**
**salt to taste**
**500ml (16fl oz) chicken stock**
**50ml (2fl oz) dry sherry**

Preheat oven to 200ºC (400ºF, Gas Mark 6).

Place bulb of garlic on a baking tray with a splash of oil and put in oven for 4 minutes.

Heat 200ml olive oil in a heavy iron pan. Put the sliced potatoes in the pan, season with 1 teaspoon salt and toss once in the oil. Reduce the heat and fry the potatoes for 15 to 20 minutes. Drain off the surplus oil. Beat the eggs with a teaspoon of salt. Carefully fold in the sliced potatoes and then leave the entire mixture to rest for a while, about 2 minutes.

Heat the remaining oil in the pan and put the potato and egg mixture into it. Smooth it out and let it thicken for a few minutes on low heat. Turn the potato omelette over with the help of a plate or a lid and brown it in the same way on the other side. In a saucepan, reduce chicken stock and sherry by half. Serve topped with roasted garlic, spoon over the dry sherry sauce and splash with olive oil.

**To Drink**
The fruity, dark cherry, nutty flavours of Tempranillo enhances this traditional Spanish dish. Our Brandy Creek 2008 Tempranillo grapes were picked a little earlier than our previous Tempranillos, resulting in a softening of the tannins.

# View Café Orange Blossom Salad

Serves 2

200g (7oz) rocket (arugula) leaves
100g (3½oz) iceberg lettuce
1 orange, segmented
¼ red onion, sliced
6 cornichons (gherkins)
scooped out fruit of 1 pomegranate
6 walnut halves

Orange Blossom Dressing (see page 152)

Put all ingredients in a bowl and toss lightly.

Place on a plate and dress with Orange Blossom Dressing.

**To Drink**
Pinot Gris has tropical fruit and mineral flavours strong enough to compete with the citrus of this salad. 2009 was a hot year that produced a full-flavoured Pinot Gris for Brandy Creek Wines.

# Grilled Field Mushrooms with Hazelnut Gremolata

Serves 3

Gremolata
**2 cups hazelnuts, coarsely chopped**
**2 cloves garlic, finely chopped**
**¼ cup parsley, finely chopped**
**2 tablespoons lemon zest**
**salt and freshly ground pepper**

**6 medium field mushrooms**
**olive oil**

Combine hazelnuts, garlic, parsley and lemon zest in a medium bowl and season with salt and pepper to taste.

Brush mushrooms on both sides with olive oil and season with salt and pepper to taste. Grill (broil) for 5 to 6 minutes on each side until just cooked through. Sprinkle with the gremolata, and serve immediately.

**To Drink**
Pinot Noir. Brandy Creek Wines 2005 Pinot Noir is a light summer-style pinot that will sit behind and enhance the flavours of this dish.

# Broad Beans with Garlic & Chilli

olive oil
300g (10oz) broad beans, shelled
2 cloves garlic, sliced
1 red chilli, sliced
salt
lemon wedges

Heat the olive oil in a pan, toss in the broad beans and gently sauté. Add sliced garlic and chilli, toss in pan and add salt to taste.

Serve immediately with lemon wedges if desired.

**To Drink**
Pinot Noir. Brandy Creek Wines 2006 Pinot Noir is more delicate than the robust 2007; its earthy, gamy, savoury tones highlight the more delicate flavours of this dish.

# Braised Kipler Potatoes with Green Olives & Pangritata

Serves 4

500g (1.1lb) kipfler potatoes
300ml (10fl oz) chicken stock
1 tablespoon green olive cheeks
1 teaspoon mint
1 teaspoon parsley
1 teaspoon sherry vinegar
1 teaspoon butter

Pangritata
2 slices stale white bread, cut into cubes
2 tablespoons olive oil
lemon zest
sprig of thyme
salt and pepper

Preheat oven to 165ºC (325ºF, Gas Mark 3).

For the Pangritata, put the bread on an oven tray, with the olive oil, lemon zest, thyme (without the stem), salt and pepper and bake until golden brown, about 6 minutes.

Bring potatoes to the boil in the chicken stock and boil until tender, then drain. Remove the potatoes and bring stock to the boil until it is reduced by one-third. Add the cooked kipflers, olive cheeks, a leaf of torn mint, chopped parsley, sherry vinegar, butter, salt and pepper. Simmer for one minute and serve in a bowl topped with a little of the Pangritata.

**To Drink**
Pinot Noir goes well with the kipflers. Brandy Creek Wines 2005 Pinot Noir has developed a nuttier flavour, reflecting the effects of barrel treatment and its bottle age.

# Button Mushrooms Stuffed with Béchamel Sauce & Jamon

Serves 5

30g (1oz) butter, chopped
45g (1½oz) plain flour
2½ cups (600ml, 20fl oz) milk
75g (2½oz) jamon, chopped
pinch salt
pinch ground nutmeg
25 button mushrooms, good-sized
¹/₃ cup breadcrumbs
pinch of pimenton

Preheat oven to 180ºC (350ºF, Gas Mark 4).

Melt butter in a medium saucepan over medium-high heat until foaming.

Add flour. Cook, stirring, for 1 to 2 minutes or until bubbling. Remove from heat. Slowly add milk, whisking constantly, until mixture is smooth. Return to heat. Cook, stirring with a wooden spoon, for 10 to 12 minutes or until sauce comes to the boil, thickens and coats the back of a wooden spoon. Remove from heat. Stir in jamon, salt and nutmeg.

Pluck stem from mushrooms and fill mushroom heads with jamon and béchamel sauce. Sprinkle with breadcrumbs and bake in the oven for 5 minutes.

Sprinkle with pimenton, serve immediately

**To Drink**
The earthy, forest floor, barnyard flavours of Pinot Noir just cry out for mushrooms and jamon. The Brandy Creek 2007 Pinot Noir is a little heavier in style than our previous pinot noirs.

# View Café Dukkah

Serves 20

160g (5½oz) sesame seeds
120g (4oz) hazelnuts
2 tablespoons coriander seeds
2 tablespoons cumin seeds
¼ teaspoon salt
¼ teaspoon pepper

Preheat oven to 180ºC (350ºF, Gas Mark 4).

Spread sesame seeds on a baking tray. Roast for 10–12 minutes or until golden brown. Transfer to a flat tray to cool. Spread hazelnuts on tray. Roast for 10 minutes until skins turn brown. Rub off skins with tea towel. Chop the nuts finely.

Place coriander and cumin seeds in a small frying pan. Dry-fry over medium heat for 5 minutes or until toasted and aromatic.

Mix sesame, hazelnuts, coriander seeds, cumin seeds, salt and pepper together.

Store in an airtight container until ready to use.

# Bread & Tomatoes

Serves 6

4 firm-fleshed tomatoes, peeled and chopped
2 cloves garlic, thinly sliced
1 tablespoon yellow mustard seeds
2 tablespoons olive oil
1 tablespoon chopped parsley
salt to taste
crusty bread

Place chopped tomatoes, sliced garlic, mustard seeds, olive oil and chopped parsley in a bowl and mix together gently. Add salt to taste.

Spread on crusty bread and serve immediately.

# Marinated Olives

500g (1.1lb) green and black olives
200g (7oz) extra virgin olive oil
4 cloves garlic
3 sprigs thyme
3 whole red chillies, split
zest of 1 orange
2 tablespoons fennel seeds
2 tablespoons pink peppercorns
2 bay leaves

Place olives in a ceramic jar and set aside.

In a small saucepan, combine oil, garlic, thyme, red chillies, orange peel, fennel seeds, pink peppercorns and bay leaves and heat on low heat for 15 minutes. Pour over olives.

Turn a few times to distribute; let the mixture cool to room temperature.

Store in the fridge in an airtight container for up to 2 weeks.

Serve at room temperature.

# Smoky Fried Almonds

Serves 6

**2 cups blanched almonds**
**1 tablespoon salt flakes**
**1 teaspoon smoked paprika**
**oil for deep frying**

Heat oil to 180°C (350°F, Gas Mark 4).

Place almonds in a wire basket and then into the oil. Deep-fry until golden brown.

Remove from the oil, spread out on absorbent paper to cool.

Toss through salt flakes and paprika. Store in an airtight container until ready to use.

# Gazpacho

Serves 4

1 teaspoon smoked paprika
60g (2 oz) stale white bread
1 tablespoon olive oil
1 small red onion
½ cucumber, peeled and seeded
6 peeled tomatoes, deseeded
2 cloves garlic, finely chopped
2 tablespoons sherry vinegar
1 teaspoon sugar
salt and freshly ground black pepper
extra cucumber and peeled tomato, diced
ice
garlic croutons
Piquillo Pepper Sauce (see page 148)

Place smoked paprika, stale white bread, olive oil, red onion, cucumber, tomatoes and garlic into a food processor and blend until all ingredients are combined. Add vinegar and sugar.

Add extra diced cucumber and tomato, to give a chunky effect. Season to taste with salt and pepper.

Pour into a chilled glass over ice, garnish with garlic croutons and a splash of Piquillo Pepper Sauce.

Vegetables

# Sweet Corn, Cheese and Leek Empanadas

Serves 12

½ finely chopped leek, white part only
3 cloves garlic crushed
2 bay leaves
2 corn cobs, kernels removed
2 cups tasty cheese, grated
½ cup heavy cream

Shortcrust Pastry (see page 154)
salt and cracked pepper to taste
egg for pastry
olive oil for deep frying
dash of olive and chopped parsley for garnish

Heat a non-stick frying pan until hot, add the leek, garlic and bay leaves. Lightly sauté until the leek is transparent, about 5 minutes, and add the corn kernels. Toss until well combined.

Remove the bay leaves then add the cheese and cream, combining altogether. Remove from heat, cool, cover and refrigerate until ready for use.

Divide the shortcrust pastry dough in small balls the size of half an egg. Roll with a rolling pin as thinly as possible without the dough tearing, making a rounded shape from each ball.

Spoon the filling onto one half of each circle, leaving room to fold in the other half. Lightly brush the unfilled half of each circle with beaten egg. Fold over to make a half circle and seal by turning it upwards and pressing with your fingers.

Preheat oil in a heavy based pan. Deep fry the empanadas in the oil, turning each one after a few minutes. Remove from oil with slotted spoon. Drain on paper towels.

Give the plate a splash of olive oil, place empanadas on top, sprinkle with chopped parsley and serve immediately.


**To Drink**
Brandy Creek Wines 2006 Oaked Chardonnay. Not as powerful as the 2007 chardonnay, this wine is a delightful adjunct to the lighter flavours of these vegetarian empandadas

# Yoghurt Mint Dip

Serves 4

**500g (1.1lb) yoghurt**
**mint, chopped (enough to season)**
**salt to taste**
**sugar to taste**
**4 tablespoons cumin seeds**
**4 tablespoons ground cumin**
**1½ cups olive oil**
**hot toasted bread to serve**

Put the yoghurt and mint in a bowl and add salt to taste. Add a little sugar to neutralise the acid and to give the mint a good colour.

Rinse out a new piece of muslin cloth and line a sieve with it. Pour the seasoned yoghurt into the lined sieve and drain into a bowl overnight in the fridge.

Heat a small pan and dry-roast the cumin seeds till fragrant, reserve until needed. In the same pan roast the ground cumin till fragrant.

In a small frying pan gently heat the oil and when it is warm, add ground cumin and seeds and let steep over a very low flame for 8 minutes.

Turn off the heat and let cool, transfer to a jar until needed, keep refrigerated.

To serve yoghurt, spoon into bowls and top with with a dessertspoon of cumin oil. Use a knife to spread onto hot crusty bread.

# Marinated Beetroot with Anchovy, Balsamic Reduction & Rocket

Serves 2

2 baby beetroots, cooked and peeled
olive oil
red wine vinegar
2 fresh anchovy fillets in olive oil
¼ cup rocket (arugula) leaves
salt and pepper
Balsamic Reduction (see page 156)
a dollop of Piquillo Pepper Sauce (see page148)

Slice beetroots and marinate in three parts olive oil to one part red wine vinegar overnight.

Neatly arrange baby beetroot with anchovy fillets on top.

In a small bowl take some rocket and dress with red wine vinegar.

Spoon over Balsamic Reduction. Serve immediately with rocket topped with a dollop of Pequillo Pepper Sauce.

**To Drink**
Cabernet Sauvignon. The Brandy Creek Wines 2005 Cabernet Sauvignon is a medium-bodied, cool-climate cabernet with herbal, briary and blackberry characteristics would accompany the rocket and beetroot aspects of this dish.

# Fish & Seafood

# Prawns (shrimp) in Garlic & Oil

Serves 1

100g (3½oz) fresh prawns (shrimp)
2 tablespoons olive oil
1 clove garlic, crushed
salt to taste
1 red chilli
½ tablespoon chopped parsley

Heat the oil in a small frying pan. When hot, add the prawns and garlic and cook until they turn opaque. As soon as the oil is bubbling, add salt to taste. Garnish with chilli and parsley. Serve immediately.

**To Drink**
Sparkling Pinot Gris. Brandy Creek Wines 2005 version is a light and crisp early disgorged sparkling wine. It has a pronounced green-apple nose and won the best sparkling wine at two wine shows recently.

# Blue Cheese & Anchovy Tartlets

Serves 2

100g (3½oz) blue vein cheese
100ml (3½fl oz) double cream
Puff Pastry (see page 155)
6 Marinated White Anchovies (see page 75)
pink peppercorns
olive oil to garnish

Preheat oven to 180ºC (350ºF, Gas Mark 4). Combine blue cheese and cream in a bowl. Mix together to form a paste, set aside.

Roll the pastry out on a floured surface and cut into 6 circles using a round cookie cutter. Place on a baking sheet and bake tarts for 8 minutes or until pale golden in colour. Remove from oven and cool.

Place tarts on a plate, top with blue cheese paste and white anchovies. Drizzle with olive oil and sprinkle with pink peppercorns.

**To Drink**
Sauvignon Blanc. 2009 was an exceptional year for Brandy Creek Wines. Our Sauvignon Blanc has wonderful passionfruit and melon tones with a steely mouth feel to balance the anchovies.

# Anchovy & Piquillo Toasts

Serves 2

2 red piquillo peppers
4 Marinated White Anchovies (see page 75)
4 toasted bread rounds
olive oil to drizzle

Cut the piquillo peppers in 4 equal parts. Place 1 anchovy inside the piquillo pepper and roll into a cylinder shape, repeat for the other 3.

Place each piquillo roll with the open end downwards on top of the bread rounds and drizzle with olive oil. Serve immediately.

**To Drink**
Sauvignon Blanc. 2009 was an exceptional year for Brandy Creek Wines. Our Sauvignon Blanc has wonderful passionfruit and melon tones with a steely mouth feel to balance the seafood flavours of salmon and anchovy.

# Salt Cod & Potato Fritters

Serves 4

350g (12oz) potatoes
350g (12oz) salt cod, soaked overnight and rinsed
 well several times, then de-boned
1 medium onion, finely diced
1 tablespoon parsley
2 large eggs
oil for deep-frying
red chilli, chopped, for garnish
flaked salt, for garnish

Peel and boil the potatoes in plenty of water. Remove from the heat and mash the potatoes. Add the salt cod, diced onion and parsley, then beat in the eggs.

Heat the oil in a deep pan. Drop teaspoons of the salt cod mixture into the oil, turning once. When they are brown all over, remove and drain on kitchen paper.

Sprinkle with chopped red chilli and flaked salt. Serve immediately

**To Drink**
A strongly flavoured dish like salt cod calls out for a Pinot Gris with its tropical fruit nose and steely mineral taste. Brandy Creek Wines 2007 Pinot Gris is made in the French style—a medium-bodied wine to have with food.

# Mussels with Red, Green & Yellow Capsicums

Serves 2

olive oil
½ **red capsicum (pepper)**
½ **green capsicum (pepper)**
½ **yellow capsicum (pepper)**
½ **brown onion, sliced into half-moons**
1 **ripe tomato, chopped**
1 **clove garlic, sliced**
**splash white wine**
**salt to taste**
8–10 **half-shell fresh mussels**
**parsley to garnish**

Heat oil in a pan. Add red and green capsicums, onion, chopped tomato and garlic.

Cook all together, add white wine and stir until the capsicums are tender.

Taste, add salt to season.

Toss mussels in the same pan and coat with the capsicum sauce. Pour onto plate, sprinkle with parsley and serve immediately.

**To Drink**
Sparkling Tempranillo. The Brandy Creek Wines 2008 Sparkling Tempranillo is an exciting new wine. The strong Tempranillo tannins and flavours coupled with a medium sweet dosage complement the equally strong flavours of this dish.

# Seafood Soup

Serves 2

olive oil
**4 large green prawns (shrimp)**
**2 large half-shell mussels**
**2 large scallops**
**2 pieces white flesh fish**
**Fish Stock (see page 145)**
**2 slices stale bread for garlic croutons**

Preheat oven to 180°C (350°F, Gas Mark 4).

In a heavy-based pan, over a medium to high flame, place olive oil, green prawns, mussels, scallops and white fish meat and sauté until the seafood is sealed. Pour Fish Stock over fish and reduce to a simmer for 2–3 minutes.

To make garlic croutons, lay bread flat on a baking tray, drizzle each slice with a dessertspoon of olive oil and bake until crispy, about 3 minutes.

Remove from the oven and break into bite-sized pieces. Pour into bowls, drop in garlic croutons and serve immediately.

# Marinated White Anchovies

Serves 4

1 small bunch flat leaf parsley, chopped
1 dessertspoon capers, chopped
2 cloves garlic, sliced
1 tablespoon red wine vinegar
3 tablespoons olive oil
200g (7 oz) anchovy fillets

In a bowl place the parsley, capers, garlic, red wine vinegar and olive oil and stir to combine.

Place the anchovy fillets skin side down on a ceramic dish, pour over the marinade and leave in the refrigerator for at least 24 hours before use.

Divide the mixture and serve cold.

# Prawn (shrimp) & Jamon Skewers

Serves 4

juice of 4 lemons
2 cloves garlic, crushed
250g (8oz) jamon
12 medium to large uncooked prawns (shrimp), peeled and heads removed
2 tablespoons olive oil
salt and pepper
4 skewers
chopped parsley

Marinate prawns in lemon juice and crushed garlic overnight.

Cut the jamon into strips and wrap around prawns.

Skewer 3 wrapped prawns through the fattest part of the tail for each skewer. Season with salt and pepper and drizzle with olive oil.

Either cook on a hot griddle or in a hot oven (190°C, 375°F, Gas Mark 5) on an oiled baking tray for 6–8 minutes.

Squeeze lemon juice over, sprinkle with parsley, serve immediately.

**To Drink**
Sparkling Pinot Gris. Brandy Creek Wines 2006 Sparkling Pinot Gris is a light and crisp bubbly wine with citrus and pineapple flavours to enhance both the prawns and jamon components of this dish.

# Palm Heart, Piquillo & White Anchovy Skewers

Serves 12

1 tin palm hearts, drained and cut into bite-sized pieces
12 Marinated White Anchovies (see page 75) drained
6 piquillo peppers, each sliced into 3 pieces
stuffed olives
olive oil
chopped parsley
12 skewers

Skewer a palm heart segment followed by a piquillo then an anchovy and finish off with a stuffed olive. Repeat with the remaining hearts, piquillos, anchovies and stuffed olives.

Drizzle with olive oil and chopped parsley to serve.

**To Drink**
Unwooded Chardonnay. The Brandy Creek Wines 2008 Unwooded Chardonnay is simple clean and crisp with lots of well-rounded acid, and is a perfect foil for this type of seafood and marinated vegetable dish.

# Anchovy & Caviar Toasts

Serves 5

10 Marinated White Anchovies (see page 75)
bread slices, freshly toasted and cut into 10 fingers
4 teaspoons caviar

For each toast finger, lay an anchovy fillet on top then place 1 teaspoon caviar along the centre of each anchovy.

Serve immediately.

**To Drink**
Unwooded Chardonnay. The Brandy Creek Wines 2008 Unwooded Chardonnay is simple, clean and crisp, with lots of well-rounded acid. It is a perfect foil for this type of seafood dish.

# Salt Cod Puffs

Serves 8

400g (13oz) salt cod (soaked overnight and rinsed in plenty of cold water)
oil for frying
1 red capsicum (pepper), sliced
1 green capsicum, (pepper) sliced
1 yellow capsicum, (pepper) sliced
2 cloves garlic, crushed
2 tablespoons dry sherry
250g (8oz) Puff Pastry (see page 155)
olive oil to garnish

Preheat oven to 200°C (400°F, Gas Mark 6).

Heat the oil in a heavy-based pan and add the red and green capsicums and garlic. Sauté until soft, about 2 minutes, then remove from pan and set aside.

In the same pan add a little more oil, dry sherry and add the salt cod and gently cook for about 5 minutes. Remove the fish and gently flake and remove the bones at the same time.

Cut the pastry into squares and bake for 4–6 minutes or until the pastry has risen. Allow to cool.

Place flaked salt cod onto each tartlet and top with capsicums. Sprinkle with olive oil. Serve immediately.

**To Drink**
A strongly flavoured dish like salt cod calls for a Pinot Gris, with its tropical fruit nose and steely mineral taste. Brandy Creek Wines 2007 Pinot Gris is made in the French style—a medium bodied wine to have with food.

# Clams with Artichokes & Jamon

Serves 2

2 cloves garlic, finely chopped
2 tablespoons olive oil
2 slices jamon, chopped
1 cup (250ml, 8fl oz) vegetable or fish stock
2 tablespoons dry, white wine
24 clams, cleaned
10 preserved artichoke hearts, drained
2 tablespoons butter
chopped parsley

Brown the garlic cloves in hot oil in a deep frying pan or earthenware dish, add the jamon and lightly sauté. Add the white wine and stock, then toss in the clams and cook until they open. Then add the artichoke hearts and cook for a few minutes, toss in butter before serving. Serve in a cazuella, sprinkle with chopped parsley.

**To Drink**
The earthy, gamy, savoury tones of Pinot Noir highlight the more delicate flavours of this dish. Brandy Creek Wines 2006 Pinot Noir is a more delicate pinot noir than the robust 2007.

# Octopus in Paprika Sauce

Serves 4

1kg (2.2lb) octopus
1 tablespoon garlic, chopped
3 tablespoons olive oil
4 spring onions, chopped
1 tablespoon spanish sweet paprika
200ml (7fl oz) white wine
200ml (7fl oz) water
100ml (3½fl oz) chicken stock
2 tablespoons extra virgin olive oil

Clean octopus, chargrill and chop into small pieces, put aside.

In a pan, fry garlic in oil until pale gold then add shallots and cook until transparent and with a little colour.

Add paprika, cook very slowly for three minutes until you smell paprika roasting. Add octopus to shallot mix, deglaze with white wine, and reduce until there is no alcohol, then add water, cover and braise for 45 minutes on a slow heat.

Then add chicken stock, reduce to sauce consistency, and add two tablespoons extra virgin olive oil. Adjust seasoning to taste. Sprinkle with spring onions and serve immediatley.

**To Drink**
Pinot Gris. The Brandy Creek Wines 2006 Pinot Gris is a great accompaniment to this seafood dish.

# Marinated Whole Sardines

Serves 5

10 fresh sardines, cleaned but with heads left on
¼ cup salt
4 cups water
¼ cup olive oil (good quality)
2 cloves garlic, crushed
2 chillies, cut lengthwise
3 bay leaves

1 white onion, sliced
1 teaspoon thyme leaves
1 teaspoon black peppercorns
3 cups white wine
3 cups white wine vinegar
juice from one lemon
crusty bread

Mix the salt and water together to make a salt brine, place sardines in the mixture for 45 minutes.

Preheat oven to 200°C (400°F, Gas Mark 6).

Heat the oil in a heavy-based pan add the garlic, chillies and bay leaves, cook until the garlic starts to brown, about 3 minutes, add onion, thyme leaves, black peppercorns, white wine, white wine vinegar and lemon juice, simmer and reduce by half. Set aside to cool.

Place sardines on a baking tray and place in oven for 4 minutes, remove from the oven and rest.

When everything is at room temperature pour the reduced sauce over the sardines, making sure the fish are covered.

Just before serving, gently heat and place on crusty bread.

This dish will keep in an airtight container in the fridge for up to a week.


**To Drink**
Shiraz. The sardines with the garlic and chilli sauce are strongly flavoured and somewhat oily. They demand a robust wine. Brandy Creek Wines 2006 Shiraz (Longford Vineyard) is a French-style Shiraz, which won best shiraz at the International Cool Climate Wine Show in 2008.

# Deep-Fried Whitebait

Serves 2

300g (10oz) fresh whitebait (smelt)
plain flour
vegetable oil for frying
salt flakes
lemon wedges

Dust the whitebait with the flour.

Heat the vegetable oil to 180ºC (350ºF, Gas Mark 4). Deep-fry the whitebait until golden and crispy or until they begin to float in the oil.

Drain on paper towels then toss with salt flakes.

Serve hot with lemon wedges.

**To Drink**
Sauvignon Blanc. The popular Brandy Creek Wines 2008 Sauvignon Blanc features a grassy nose and a mineral taste that will enhance the whitebait.

# Beer-Battered Shrimp with Alioli

Serves 2

300g (10 oz) plain flour
salt flakes to taste
1 tablespoon olive oil
275ml (9fl oz) beer
oil for frying
2 egg whites
250g (8oz) shrimp, peeled with tails left on
Alioli (see page 147)

Sieve the flour into a bowl and add a pinch of salt. Add 1 tablespoon of olive oil and the beer. Stir the mixture well, working it from the centre outwards until it has a smooth consistency. Put aside at room temperature for 30 minutes.

Whisk the egg whites until stiff, then add to the batter.

Heat enough oil in a pan to deep-fry the shrimp. Place the shrimp in the batter one by one and fry them a few at a time until the batter has turned golden and the shrimp are done.

Serve with Alioli.

**To Drink**
Rosé. Brandy Creek Wines 2007 Rosé is made from Pinot Noir grapes with an undertone of cherry or strawberry flavour. Nice on a summer's day with the shrimp.

# Calamari Marinated in Chilli & Garlic

Serves 2

250g (8oz) calamari (squid tubes)
2 hot red chillies, chopped
2 cloves garlic, chopped
¼ cup olive oil
salt to taste
lemon wedges
parsley for garnish

Clean the calamari, removing the tendrils and wings. Cut the tube in half along the spine. Using the back of your knife, scrape the tube clean. Repeat this for the other tubes. Once you have all tubes clean, score the inside of the tube in a crisscross pattern. Cut crossways into thick strips.

Place calamari, chilli, garlic and olive oil in a large ceramic bowl. Stir together and let marinate in the refrigerator for 2 hours.

Preheat a greased barbecue plate on high heat, add calamari and cook for 1 to 2 minutes each side, or until curled and just cooked through.

Serve immediately with a wedge of lemon, and sprinkle of parsley.

**To Drink**
Oaked Chardonnay. Described by many judges as 'the complete' chardonnay, Brandy Creek Wines 2007 Oaked Chardonnay has beautiful butter/butterscotch flavours from the French oak and delicate smoky peach and nectarine characteristics. This wine has the flavour and strength to enhance this dish.

# Meat

# Dates with Blue Cheese, Red Chilli & Jamon

Serves 4

300ml (10fl oz) cream sherry
12 fresh medjool dates, seeded
200g (7oz) cabrales cheese, or other blue cheese
6 red chillies, cut in half lengthways
12 slices jamon
olive oil for brushing

Marinate dates overnight in cream sherry.

Preheat oven to 180°C (350°F, Gas Mark 4).

Drain the dates and fill the cavities of the dates with about half a teaspoon blue cheese and place one half of a chilli into each date. Take a slice of jamon and wrap each date tightly.

Place them on a baking sheet, brush with olive oil and bake for 3–5 minutes. Serve immediately.

**To Drink**
Tempranillo. Brandy Creek Wines 2004 Reserve Tempranillo is made from carefully selected grapes from our first vintage. The huge Tempranillo tannins in this wine have softened with age to produce a wonderful savoury wine that complements magically the strong flavours of this dish.

# Chorizo Cooked in Red Wine with Pimenton

Serves 2

2 chorizo sausages
¾ cup (185ml, 6fl oz) robust red wine
1 roasted red capsicum (pepper), cut into slices
2 cloves garlic, minced
1 tablespoon parsley, chopped

Brown the sausage in a frying pan, then remove it and deglaze the juices with half of the red wine. Burn off the alcohol and let it simmer for 2 minutes.

Add the roasted red capsicum and minced garlic. When it has bubbled for 1 minute add chopped parsley and the sausages and cook for a further 5 minutes.

Remove from heat and serve immediately.

**To Drink**
Tempranillo. Brandy Creek Wines 2007 Tempranillo features strong mouth-puckering tannins with plenty of herbal and spicy characteristics for which it is famous. An excellent year to complement full-flavoured chorizo.

# Jamon Croquetas

Serves 6

**3 tablespoons olive oil**
**½ onion, minced**
**4 tablespoons plain flour**
**1 cup (250ml, 8fl oz) milk**
**pinch sweet pimenton**
**salt and pepper**
**3 slices jamon, diced**
**2 eggs, beaten with a little water**
**2 cups breadcrumbs**
**olive oil for frying**

Heat the oil in a pan and sauté minced onion until transparent. Stir in the flour and cook it briefly, then whisk in the milk. Cook, stirring constantly until the sauce thickens. Season with salt, pepper and pimenton. Stir in the jamon and spread the mixture into a dish. Refrigerate until solid.

Place the beaten eggs in one dish, the breadcrumbs in another. With moistened hands, form the chilled mixture into balls or cylinders. Dip each croquet first in flour, then in beaten egg, then in breadcrumbs, taking care that they are well covered.

Heat olive oil in a deep fryer and fry the croquetas a few at a time, until golden, about 3 minutes.

**To Drink**
Pinot Noir. A more delicate pinot noir than the robust 2007, Brandy Creek Wines 2006 Pinot Noir has earthy, gamy, savoury tones highlight the more delicate flavours of this dish.

# Provincial Meatballs

Serves 8

**2 slices stale bread**
**1 cup (250ml, 8fl oz) milk**
**750g (1½lb) lean beef mince (ground)**
**250g (8oz) shoulder pork mince (ground)**
**2 medium-sized onions, peeled and diced**
**chopped parsley**
**2 eggs**
**½ cup (125ml, 4fl oz) white wine**
**oil for frying**
**Tomato Sauce (see page 142)**
**dollop of Yoghurt Mint Dip (see page 55)**
**chilli and parsley for garnish**

Soak the bread in milk while you get everything together. When the milk has been absorbed, mash with a fork.

In a bowl, place beef mince, pork mince, diced onions, parsley and eggs, then add the bread and white wine.

Mix together to form small bite-sized balls. Fry in hot oil until brown, transfer to a heatproof dish.

Serve hot with Tomato Sauce and Yoghurt Mint Dip on the top and garnish with chilli and parsley.

**To Drink**
Shiraz. The Brandy Creek Wines 2006 Shiraz (Bairnsdale Vineyard) is a balanced shiraz with nice white pepper, berry fruits and plums. Great with meatballs.

# Brandy Creek Quail with Grapes & Sherry

Serves 2

1 quail, halved
200ml (7fl oz) sherry
50ml (2fl oz) grape juice
1L (34fl oz) chicken stock
1 red onion, chopped
1 large clove garlic
2 tablespoons olive oil
1 teaspoon parsley, chopped
10 grapes, cut in half
salt and pepper

Barbecue or grill the quail.

Put sherry in saucepan and burn off alcohol. Add grape juice and chicken stock and reduce by half. Add chopped red onion, garlic, olive oil and parsley, season and then add grapes.

To serve, put chargrilled quail on a plate and pour a little of the sauce over it.

**To Drink**
Pinot Noir. Brandy Creek Wines 2006 Pinot Noir is a delicate pinot noir; its earthy, gamy, savoury tones blend with and highlight the also delicate flavours of the quail.

# Roasted Pork Belly with Fennel

Serves 4

1 tablespoon cooking salt
¼ cup (60ml, 2fl oz) olive oil
1 tablespoon fennel seeds
1 fennel bulb, sliced
500g (1.1lb) pork belly in one piece

Preheat oven to 230°C (450°F, Gas Mark 8).

Combine the salt, oil and fennel seeds in a bowl.

Place the pork on a clean flat surface, skin side up. With a sharp knife, score the belly about one centimetre (about an ½ inch) apart through the skin into the fat. Using your hands, rub the fennel mixture over the pork and push it into the scored skin.

Season bottom of pork with salt and pepper, place belly into a baking tray and bake for 30 minutes. Take the pork out and drain rendered fat, place pork on a roasting rack and then back in tray and add 2 cups of water. Reduce heat to 165°C (325°F, Gas Mark 3) and cook for a further 2 hours. In the final half hour of baking, place sliced fennel around the pork belly and bake until it has wilted.

Remove from oven, cut pork into strips and serve on a bed of fennel.

**To Drink**
Pinot Gris. Brandy Creek Wines 2007 Late Harvest Pinot Gris is a medium-weight sweet wine. The stone fruit and pear overtones pick up both the pork and fennel from this very popular dish.

# Hot Wings

Serves 2

**300g (10oz) chicken wings, cut in half**
**sea salt**
**olive oil for deep-frying**
**Peri Peri Sauce (see page 150)**
**2 sticks celery**
**Yoghurt Mint Dip (see page 55)**

Place the chicken wings in a wire basket and toss with salt.

Deep-fry the wings in boiling olive oil. Remove from the oil and drain.

Place Peri Peri Sauce in shallow frying pan, place wings into pan and coat with the sauce and reheat.

Place chicken on a serving dish with Yoghurt Mint Dip and celery sticks.

**To Drink**
Sparkling Wine or Champagne. Brandy Creek 2006 Menage a Trois Sparkling Wine is made from the three traditional French Champagne grapes and this creamy, yeast-flavoured late disgorged sparkling wine will balance the heat of this popular dish.

# Honey-Baked Chicken Thighs

Serves 3

50g (2 oz) honey
450ml (15 fl oz) Tomato Sauce (see page 142)
40g (1 oz) butter
1 tablespoon smoky pimenton
6 chicken thighs

Preheat oven to 180ºC (350ºF, Gas Mark 4).

Place all the ingredients except the chicken in a saucepan and heat over a low temperature until combined. Mix well and reduce liquid for approximately 2 minutes.

Roll the chicken thighs and place in a baking dish, pour the sauce over them and bake in the oven for 30 minutes or until the chicken is dark and glossy.

Serve immediately.

**To Drink**
Oaked Chardonnay has the flavour and strength to enhance this dish. Brandy Creek Wines 2007 Oaked Chardonnay is described by many judges as 'the complete' chardonnay, with beautiful butter/butterscotch flavours from the French oak and delicate smoky peach and nectarine characteristics.

# Sweets

# View Café Valencia Cake

4 eggs
½ cup sugar
1 cup flour
2 tablespoons butter, melted

Filling
6 oranges
3 tablespoons gelatine
4 tablespoons hot water
200g (7oz) caster sugar
2 cups natural yoghurt
2 teaspoons lemon juice
2 cups whipped cream

Topping
600ml (20fl oz, 1¼pints) orange juice (no pulp)
3 tablespoons caster sugar
9 teaspoons cornflour (cornstarch)

Preheat oven to 180°C (350°F, Gas Mark 4).

Cream together eggs and sugar until light and fluffy—about 3 minutes. Gradually mix in flour, then the melted butter. Pour into a greased 20cm (8 inch) tin. Bake for 25 minutes till it springs back when touched. Cool.

When cool, lay sponge cake in the bottom of a springform pan. Cut 2 oranges into rounds and place orange rounds around inside of springform pan. Process remaining 4 oranges to a medium consistency and drain the juice.

Dissolve gelatine in water and mix together with sugar, yoghurt, puréed oranges and lemon juice. Fold in whipped cream and pour into the tin. Leave to set, for approximately 45 minutes in refrigerator.

Combine all the topping ingredients in a saucepan, stir until boiling, allow to cool. Pour over filling, chill for about 1 hour. Cut into wedges to serve.

**To Drink**
Liqueur Sauvingnon Blanc. Brandy Creek Wines Liqueur Sauvignon Blanc is a little bittersweet and it really picks up the orange in this great dessert.

# The Drunken Spanish Cake

4 eggs
½ cup sugar
1 cup flour
2 tablespoons butter, melted

Syrup
6 tablespoons white sugar
6 tablespoons water
1 cinnamon stick
5 tablespoons rum
4 tablespoons Grand Marnier

Custard filling
1½ cups cow's milk
zest of 1 lemon
3 egg yolks
¼ cup caster sugar
¼ cup plain flour
2 teaspoons butter

icing sugar to serve

Preheat oven to 180°C (350°F, Gas Mark 4).

Cream together eggs and sugar until light and fluffy— about 3 minutes.

Gradually mix in flour, then the melted butter. Pour into a greased 20cm (8 inch) tin.

Bake for 25 minutes till it springs back when touched. Cool.

Place all the syrup ingredients in a saucepan and bring to boil. Pour half the syrup over the sponge while still warm. Turn out and pour the rest over the other side.

For the custard, heat the milk with the lemon zest to boiling point. Reduce the heat and simmer for 10 minutes. Discard the zest. In a heavy pan, whip the egg yolks and the sugar. Add the flour and mix until smooth. Add the milk a little at a time. Cook over a moderate heat, stir constantly until mixture boils and no flour taste remains,  about 2 or 3 minutes. Cool, stirring to stop a skin forming. Split the sponge in half and fill with the custard.

Dredge with icing sugar and serve immediately.

**To Drink**
Liqueur Pinot Gris. Brandy Creek Wines Liqueur Pinot Gris, with its flavours of apricots, pears and tangerines is a perfect partner for this dessert.

# Vanilla Bean Ice-Cream

Makes 2½ litres

1L (34fl oz) cream
1L (34fl oz) cow's milk
3 vanilla beans, split and scraped, retain seeds
20 egg yolks
400g (13oz) caster sugar

Pour cream and milk into a large boiler add the vanilla bean seeds and pods.

Bring to the boil, remove from the heat and allow the vanilla to infuse for 40 minutes.

Beat the egg yolks with the sugar to form a 'ribbon'. Pour over the cream and mix well.

Strain the liquid back into the pot and cook over a moderate heat, stirring continuously, until the mixture begins to thicken and coats the back of a wooden spoon (temperature must reach 80°C, 200°F on thermostat or kitchen thermometer). Cool and pour into an ice-cream churn and churn to freeze. Once frozen, scoop into a tray and place in freezer.

**To Drink**
Liqueur Chardonnay. Brandy Creek Wines Liqueur Chardonnay is smooth and sweet with a toffee taste. Don't just sip it from the glass—pour it on top of the ice-cream!

# Dulce De Leche Ice-Cream

Makes 3 litres

**2 x 395ml tins condensed milk**
**2½ litres vanilla ice-cream**

Place tins into a large boiler, cover with water and simmer for four hours (continually add water to the boiler, making sure tins are always covered with water) then remove and set aside to cool.

Once condensed milk is cold, open tins and mix through vanilla ice-cream— do this quickly for the ice-cream to remain frozen. Place back in freezer until needed.

**To Drink**
Liqueur Pinot Gris. Brandy Creek Wines Liqueur Pinot Gris is a sweet -liqueur tasting of apricots, pears and tangerine has strong enough flavours to add to this dessert.

# Crema Catalana

Serves 4

**4 egg yolks**
**1 cup sugar**
**1 stick cinnamon**
**zest from 1 lemon**
**2 cups (500ml, 17 fl oz) warm milk**
**1 tablespoon cornflour (cornstarch)**

Beat egg yolks and ¼ cup of sugar until frothy. Add the cinnamon, lemon and cornflour then pour on the warm milk. Slowly heat the mixture, stirring until it begins to thicken and boil. Turn off the heat, and divide between heatproof dishes.

Sprinkle the remaining sugar on top of the custard and scorch with a gas gun or place under a grill (broiler) to melt.

**To Drink**
Brandy Creek Wines Liqueur Chardonnay. Smooth and sweet with a toffee taste.

# Red Wine Sorbet

Serves 4

1L (34fl oz) red wine
150g (5oz) caster sugar
8 cloves
8 white peppercorns
zest 2 oranges

Place the wine, sugar, cloves, peppercorns and orange zest into a saucepan and boil, reducing by half. When cool, strain and pour into an ice-cream churn, churn until frozen. Scoop into tray and place in freezer.

Sorbet can be served with summer berries, strawberries or raspberries.

**To Drink**
Sparkling Shiraz. Brandy Creek Wines Sparkling Shiraz is bursting with tiny bubbles of perfect shiraz characteristics (plums, leather, some liquorice, lots of spice).

# Baked Quince

Serves 2

2 large ripe quince
200g (7oz) sugar
2 tablespoons honey
1 cup (250ml, 8fl oz) water

Chantilly Cream
½ cup (120ml, 4fl oz) pouring cream
2 tablespoons caster sugar
1 tablespoon brandy

Preheat oven to 180ºC (350ºF, Gas Mark 4).

Wash quince and rub fuzzy coat from skins. Cut each quince in half and place in baking dish flesh side up. Sprinkle with sugar and honey then pour the water into the baking dish, about an inch deep.

Bake in oven for 45 minutes.

Whisk together all the Chantilly Cream ingredients until soft peaks form.

Serve quinces hot with Chantilly Cream.

**To Drink**
Brandy Creek Wines 2008 Late Harvest Pinot Gris. A perfect combination.

# Portuguese Custard Tarts

Makes 12 tarts

**Puff Pastry (see page 155)**
4 egg yolks
2 tablespoons white sugar
2 tablespoons cornflour (cornstarch)
2 cups cream
1 cup (250ml, 8 fl oz) water
2 tablespoons icing sugar to dust

Preheat oven to 180°C (350°F, Gas Mark 4).

Roll the pastry and cut into 12 discs. Grease a muffin pan, line with the discs of puff pastry, set aside.

In a small saucepan, combine egg yolks and sugar and mix to a smooth consistency, then add cornflour and again mix into a smooth paste. Gradually add the cream and water.

Cook over medium heat until mixture boils.

Pour custard into muffin pans and bake for 20 minutes. Remove tarts from pan once cooled. Dust with icing sugar and serve immediately.

**To Drink**
Liqueur Chardonnay. Smooth and sweet, Brandy Creek Wines Liqueur Chardonnay has a toffee taste that complements these tarts.

# Churros

Serves 6 (3 per serve)

zest 1 orange
1 cup (250ml, 8fl oz) water
2 tablespoons butter
1 teaspoon sugar
pinch salt
1½ cups plain flour
2 eggs
4 cups olive oil
1 tablespoon cinnamon
1 cup sugar

Bittersweet Chocolate Sauce
300g (10oz) semisweet chocolate, cut into chunks
⅓ cup (80ml, 2½fl oz) honey
1 cup (250ml, 8fl oz) pouring cream
4 tablespoons Dutch process cocoa

To make the churros, put the orange zest, water, butter, sugar and salt in a large saucepan and bring to a rapid boil, stirring constantly. Add the flour all at once and continue to cook until combined. Transfer the churros dough to a mixer fitted with a dough hook and beat in the eggs one at a time. Continue to mix until the dough forms soft peaks.

Heat the olive oil to 180°C (350°F) in a large, deep saucepan.

Transfer the dough to a piping bag with a star nozzle, big enough for the dough to flow freely. Pipe the dough into the oil in lengths about 15cm (6 inches) long. When it is golden brown all over, remove from oil and drain on paper towels.

To make the chocolate sauce, place the chocolate, honey and pouring cream in a steel bowl. Heat a saucepan of water and place the steel bowl on to the saucepan and melt the mixture. Stir until they are all combined and remove from heat.

Combine cinnamon and sugar in a tray, then dust each churros until coated. Serve immediately with the chocolate sauce.

**To Drink**
Pinot Noir. Brandy Creek Wines Liqueur Pinot Noir has classic raisin and Christmas pudding flavour, which tastes fantastic with churros.

# Sweet Apple Tart

250g (8oz) plain flour
75g (3oz) icing sugar
125g (4oz) unsalted butter, cut into cubes
1 egg
1 tablespoon chilled water
butter for greasing
500g (1.1lb) apples, peeled cored and sliced
juice 1 lemon
apricot jam for glazing

Sieve the flour into a mixing bowl then sieve the icing sugar onto the flour, drop in cubes of butter and rub the mixture together using your fingertips until the mixture resembles breadcrumbs. Add the egg and chilled water and gently work the mixture until you have a ball of dough. Wrap the dough in plastic wrap and place in refrigerator for about 30 minutes.

Preheat oven to 200°C (400°F, Gas Mark 6).

Roll out the dough. Grease your pastry tray or tart tin, and line with the pastry. Draw it up over the edges to allow for shrinkage. Prick the bottom with a fork. Arrange the apple slices on the pastry and pour the lemon juice on top. Bake in oven for 30 minutes.

Leave the tart to cool a little before brushing with the melted apricot glaze.

# Basic Essentials

# Base Tomato Sauce

Makes 2 litres

2 tablespoons olive oil
8 cloves garlic, crushed
2 onions, diced
3kg (6.6 lb) tomatoes, peeled
4 bay leaves
salt
pepper

Heat the oil in a heavy saucepan, add the garlic and onion and cook over a low heat for 20 minutes until soft but not brown.

Add the tomatoes and bay leaves and continue to cook again over a low heat for approximately 1½ hours, stirring constantly to prevent sticking to the bottom of the pan.

Season to taste.

Remove from heat, cool, store in refrigerator until needed.

# Tomato Sauce For Meatballs

Makes 8 cups

4 tablespoons olive oil
2 onions, diced
8 cloves garlic, crushed
3kg (6.6lb) tomatoes, peeled
1 tablespoon ground cumin
2 tablespoons sweet pimenton
2 tablespoons smoky pimenton
2 teaspoons cinnamon
4 bay leaves
salt to season
pepper

Pour olive oil into a large heavy-based pan and gently fry the onions and garlic together, until soft and still pale in colour. Place all the other ingredients into the pot, bring to the boil, stirring every few minutes to prevent sauce from sticking to the bottom of the pan. Cook for 1 hour until mixture thickens.

Remove from heat, cool, store in refrigerator until needed.

# Chicken Stock

Makes 6 litres

4kg (8.8lb) chicken carcases
3 leeks, roughly chopped
2 peeled whole white onions
3 large carrots, roughly chopped
½ head celery, chopped
1 bunch thyme
4 bay leaves
1 tablespoon peppercorns
10L (340fl oz, 40 cups) cold water

Place the chicken carcases, leeks, onions, carrots, celery, thyme, bay leaves, peppercorns and water into a large stockpot.

Heat over a high flame until stock begins to boil, turn the heat down to a low simmer and cook uncovered for 6 hours, periodically skimming off the foam that rises to the top.

Strain the stock through a fine sieve, let cool, cover and refrigerate until well chilled, then lift off fat and discard. Store for up to 4 days.

# Fish Stock

Makes 5 litres

**6kg (6.6 lb) fish heads**
**¼ cup olive oil**
**1 cup (250 ml, 8 fl oz) dry white wine, such as a pinot grigio**
**3 leeks, thinly sliced**
**1 head celery, sliced**
**1kg (2.2 lb) carrots, sliced into rounds**
**½ bunch parsley**
**6 bay leaves**
**1 sprig fresh thyme or 1 teaspoon dried thyme**
**8L (256fl oz; 32 cups) cold water**
**salt**

Wash fish heads well under cold water. If the gills are still attached, cut them out.

Heat a large pan for 2 minutes on high heat, and then add the oil. Turn the heat down to medium and add the fish heads. Cook, stirring frequently, for about 5 minutes. Remove and set aside.

In a tall stockpot, add the wine and reduce it by half under high heat. Once this is done, add the fish bones and turn off the heat for now. Add the leek, celery, carrots, parsley, bay leaves, thyme, water and fish. Turn the heat back on and bring to the boil. Reduce the heat and simmer for about 30 minutes, skimming any foam that floats to the top. Allow to cool, then strain.

Store in refrigerator for up to 3 days, or freeze for up to 2 months.

# Romesco Sauce

Makes 1½ cups

10 hazelnuts
10 blanched almonds
¼ cup olive oil
2 slices stale bread
5 piquillo peppers
½ teaspoon smoked sweet paprika
4 garlic cloves
1 tablespoon sherry vinegar
1 ripe tomato, peeled, seeded and chopped

Preheat oven to 200ºC (400ºF, Gas Mark 6).

Toast hazelnuts and almonds in the oven until golden, about 4 minutes, allow to cool.

Heat 2 tablespoons of the oil in a pan and fry the bread for 2 minutes. Remove and drain on paper towel and allow to cool.

In a food processor place nuts, bread, piquillo peppers, paprika, garlic cloves, sherry vinegar, tomato and remaining oil.

Blend to a paste and season to taste.

# Alioli

Makes 1 cup

**1 egg**
**2 garlic cloves, chopped**
**1 cup extra virgin olive oil**
**½ teaspoon salt**

Place the egg and chopped garlic in a blender or food processor. Whirl until garlic is smooth. With the motor running, add the oil in a slow stream, until the sauce is thick and emulsified. Add salt to taste.

# Piquillo Pepper Sauce

Makes 2 cups

2 cups piquillo peppers
2 cloves garlic, crushed
1 tablespoon olive oil
1 tablespoon sherry vinegar
1 tablespoon parsley
1 teaspoon brown sugar
salt to taste

Place all the ingredients in a food processor and mix until smooth, about 1 minute.

Store in refrigerator for up to 3 days.

Basic Essentials

*From top, clockwise, Alioli, Peri Peri Sauce, Piquillo Pepper Sauce, Romesco Sauce.*

# Peri Peri Sauce

Makes ½ cup

**12 birds' eye chillies, finely chopped**
**½ teaspoon salt**
**juice of ½ a lime**
**100ml (3½fl oz) olive oil**
**1 teaspoon garlic, crushed**

Place all ingredients in a food processor and mix until combined, about 1 minute.

Store in refrigerator for up to a week.

# Piperade

Makes 1 litre

4 tablespoons olive oil
2 small onions, peeled and diced
1 medium red bell capsicum (pepper), seeded and thinly sliced
1 medium yellow bell capsicum (pepper), seeded and thinly sliced
4 cloves garlic, thinly sliced
4 ripe tomatoes, chopped into small pieces
salt and pepper to taste
dried red chilli powder

Heat the oil in a large sauté pan over medium heat. Add the onions, capsicums, sliced garlic and chopped tomatoes and cook, stirring occasionally, for about 8 minutes or until vegetables have softened and begin to colour. Remove from the heat and set aside to cool.

Season with salt and pepper and dried red chilli. Use immediately or store in refrigerator for up to 5 days.

# Orange Blossom Dressing

1 tablespoon orange flower water
2 tablespoons lemon juice
2 tablespoons caster sugar
pinch cinnamon

Mix all the ingredients together and pour over a salad. Serve immediately.

# Shortcrust Pastry

250g (8oz) plain flour
¼ teaspoon salt
125g (4oz) unsalted butter, chilled, finely sliced
1 egg yolk
¼ cup (60ml, 2fl oz) iced water

Sift together the flour and salt, drop the butter slices into the flour. Rub together for a minute or so until the mixture resembles coarse breadcrumbs.

Make a well in the centre and add the yolk and ice water into the flour and butter mixture. Stir it very quickly with a fork, until the dough gathers together. Form the dough into a ball, wrap it in plastic wrap, and refrigerate until ready to use—at least 30 minutes.

# Puff Pastry

250g (8 oz) plain flour
¼ teaspoon salt
200g (7oz) cold butter, cut into 1cm (½inch) pieces
1¼ cups (310ml, 10fl oz) cold water
1½ teaspoons lemon juice

In a large bowl, stir together the flour and salt. Add the butter and toss to coat each piece in flour. Combine the cold water and lemon juice and add to the bowl while lightly tossing the ingredients to moisten them evenly. Form the dough into a ball.

On a lightly floured surface, roll out the dough into a rectangle about 1.5cm (½ inch) thick. Keep the edges as square as possible. Fold the dough into thirds (like a business letter). Cover with plastic wrap and refrigerate for 30 minutes.

Place the dough on the floured work surface and turn at a 90 degree angle from the last time you rolled it out. Roll again into a rectangle again and fold into thirds. If the dough is still cold and manageable, rotate and roll again, then fold into thirds, or refrigerate and continue in 30 minutes. Finish by rolling the dough out to the size of an oven tray. Place on a lightly floured baking tray and wrap in plastic. Refrigerate for at least 30 minutes before using.

# Balsamic Reduction

Makes ½ cup

2 brown onions, sliced
1 dessertspoon olive oil
⅓ cup (80ml, 2½ fl oz) balsamic vinegar
¼ cup (60ml, 2 fl oz) chicken stock
1 tablespoon butter

Place olive oil and onions in a pan, and cook for a few minutes, just until browned. Stir in the balsamic vinegar and then stir in the chicken stock. Continue to cook and stir over medium-high heat for about 5 minutes, until the sauce has reduced by half.

Remove from heat, and stir in the butter.

# Index

First published in Australia in 2010 by
New Holland Publishers (Australia) Pty Ltd
Sydney • Auckland • London • Cape Town

www.newholland.com.au

1/66 Gibbes Street Chatswood NSW 2067 Australia
218 Lake Road Northcote Auckland New Zealand
86 Edgware Road London W2 2EA United Kingdom
80 McKenzie Street Cape Town 8001 South Africa

National Library of Australia Cataloguing-in-Publication entry
McDonald, Marie
Tapas / Marie McDonald.
ISBN: 9781741109566 (hbk.)
Tapas.
Appetisers.
Cookery, Spanish
641.812

Publisher: Fiona Schultz
Publishing manager: Lliane Clarke
Project editor: Helen McGarry
Proofreader: Vicki Fisher
Designer: Tania Gomes
Photography: Graeme Gillies, Tania Gomes
Production manager: Olga Dementiev
Printer: Toppan Leefung Printing Limited